D0464653

LAW ENFORCEMENT DOGS

BY PHYLLIS RAYBIN EMERT

EDITED BY DR. HOWARD SCHROEDER
Professor in Reading and Language Arts
Dept. of Elementary Education
Mankato State University

**PRODUCED & DESIGNED BY
BAKER STREET PRODUCTIONS**

CRESTWOOD HOUSE

CIP

LIBRARY OF CONGRESS CATALOGING IN PUBLICATION DATA

Emert, Phyllis Raybin.
  Law enforcement dogs.

  (Working dogs)
  SUMMARY: Discusses the use of dogs in law enforcement throughout history, the breeds suitable for such work, and methods of training the dogs.
  1. Police dogs--Juvenile literature. 2. Police dogs--Training--Juvenile literature. (1. Police dogs. 2. Police dogs--Training) I. Schroeder, Howard. II. Baker Street Productions. III. Title. IV. Series.
HV8025.E47   1985   636.7'0886   85-21351
ISBN 0-89686-284-4 (lib. bdg.)

International Standard Book Number:	Library of Congress Catalog Card Number:
Library Binding 0-89686-284-4	85-21351

ILLUSTRATION CREDITS

Peter Hornby: Cover, 4, 7, 8, 25, 39, 40, 43
Tom Iverson/U.S. Customs Service: 12, 15
U.S. Air Force: 16
P.R. Emert: 19
J. Berke: 21, 29, 44
Russel F. Porter/Central Florida Criminal Justice
    Regional Training Center: 22, 26, 30, 31, 35, 36, 37

CRESTWOOD HOUSE
Hwy. 66 South, Box 3427
Mankato, MN 56002-3427

Table of contents

The author wishes to acknowledge the following people and organizations without whose help and cooperation this book would not have been possible:

Robert L. Cook, Canine Instructor, Central Florida Criminal Justice Regional Training Center, Orlando Florida;

Chuck Truax, Regional Canine Enforcement Program Manager, U.S. Customs Service, Los Angeles, California;

John Mason, Regional Canine Enforcement Program Supervisor, U.S. Customs Service, Los Angeles, California;

Richard Rogers, United States Police Canine Association, Upper Marlboro, Maryland. Special thanks to Rae Philbin.

Officer Josh Charles and Toby are partners.

1.

Toby and Bingo

Officer Josh Charles waved goodbye to his wife and kids. As the patrol car pulled away, he turned to his partner. "It's time for work, Toby," he said. Toby answered by wagging his tail.

Officer Charles' partner was a three-year-old German shepherd dog. They had been together for over two years. Toby lived with the Charles' family. Each day brought new and sometimes dangerous assignments. But the large brown and black shepherd was trained well. He helped Officer Charles enforce the law and catch criminals.

They had some close calls. Once Toby was shot in the side. Another time, Officer Charles was wounded in the leg. But they caught the suspects and, in a few weeks, were back on duty.

Now the two were assigned to night patrol. Police K-9's are very valuable to their partners at night. Dogs have an excellent sense of smell. It's forty times better than a person's. Their hearing is twenty times better. The dogs give their partners an important edge over criminals in the dark.

Suddenly, a voice crackled over the two-way car radio. "Car 202 and all units in the area," it said. "Go to 1246 North Elm. There's a robbery in progress at the all-night market.''

''That's us, boy,'' said Charles. He turned the car around and raced down the street. As they arrived at the market, one suspect ran to his car. He was waving a gun in the air. The man started the engine and screeched off down the street. Two deputies arrived at the same time as Officer Charles and Toby. They chased after him in their patrol car.

The other suspect ran out the back of the market. He disappeared into the night. ''They took all the money in the cash register,'' said the bleeding clerk. ''Then hit me with a gun. But I managed to press the police alarm button under the shelf.''

Backup officers and medical help arrived. Then Officer Charles and Toby took off after the suspect. Charles held Toby on a leash. The back of the market led to a dark alley. There were warehouses on both sides. ''Find him, Toby,'' said Charles.

The officer and dog walked slowly forward. Toby's nose led him directly to a partly-opened warehouse door. As the dog walked into the building, its body tensed. Toby's ears stood straight up. Officer Charles was sure the suspect was hiding in the building. Toby had sensed the person was there.

Officer Charles shouted loudly, ''This is a police officer K-9 unit. Come out or I will release my dog to come in after you.'' Charles waited but there was no

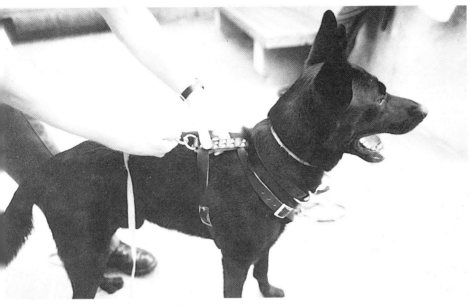
Toby's leash is unhooked.

answer. He reached down, unhooked the leash, and turned Toby loose.

The dog searched the building for the suspect. Suddenly, Charles heard growling and then a loud yelp. It sounded like his partner was in trouble. Charles rushed to see what was happening.

Toby had cornered the suspect. Charles saw that the man had a knife. He was slashing at the dog, who tried to bite and hold him. Officer Charles ran to the suspect. ''Drop the knife,'' he shouted. The man lunged at him with the knife. Charles jumped out of the way, reaching for his revolver.

7

In the few seconds it took the suspect to stab at Officer Charles, Toby leaped into the air. He grabbed the man's weapon arm with his powerful teeth. Toby bit down hard. The man screamed in pain. The knife dropped to the floor.

Toby is given a "good work" pat.

Backup officers arrived on the scene. They quickly took the suspect into custody. "Good work, Toby," said Officer Charles. He knelt down next to his partner. Toby licked his face. It was then that he saw the dog's ear had been cut by the knife. Charles took Toby to the veterinarian for treatment. He stitched and bandaged the K-9's ear. In a few days, Toby was well.

In another part of the country, a telephone call was received at a large, busy airport.

"Is Flight 982 in the air yet?" asked the person on the phone.

"Yes, Flight 982 took off fifteen minutes ago. It's due to arrive in Denver at 4 P.M." answered the airline's worker.

"Listen to me carefully. This is a warning," said the voice. "There is a bomb on that airplane. Do you understand? There's a bomb on board!"

"Who is this? Please, what is your name? Hello, hello . . ." The line went dead.

The worker for the airlines called the supervisor. The supervisor then called airport security and the control tower. "We just received a bomb threat," said the Director of Security. "Get Flight 982 back here right now. We can't take any chances."

"Call the Bomb Squad," ordered the Director. "We want a dog waiting to board when the plane touches down. Every minute counts!"

Bingo was a tan-colored German shepherd. He was a police K-9 trained to search for and find explosives.

The dog was munching on a rawhide bone when the phone from the airport rang.

"Let's get going, Bingo," said his handler, Officer Todd Brooks, as he hung up the phone. They ran to their patrol car and rushed to the airport.

Meanwhile, the pilot of Flight 982 turned the jetliner around when he heard the news from the control tower. He was an experienced pilot of many years. He kept very calm and landed the plane as smoothly as possible. They came to a stop on a runway far away from the airport buildings and other planes.

The pilot had warned the passengers to leave the plane as quickly as possible. Although everyone was afraid, there was no panic as they went out the exits. The flight crew left the aircraft last.

Now it was time for Bingo and Officer Brooks to begin their work. "Bingo, find," said Brooks. The dog began searching the front of the plane. His special nose was trained to detect any smell of explosives. He sniffed around the cockpit where the pilot and other crew members controlled the plane. He went up and down the aisles and sniffed under and around the seats.

Next, Bingo checked the front bathrooms and then the lounge area. As they made their way toward the back of the plane, Brooks checked his watch. Three minutes had passed. Time was running out. "Find, Bingo, find," he said to the shepherd.

Brooks was beginning to think the bomb threat was just another crank call. Suddenly, Bingo's ears stood up and his body seemed to tense. He was in one of the back bathrooms in the plane. Brooks was watching him closely. Explosives detector dogs alert to their handlers by sitting quietly. He knew the dog had found something.

Bingo sat down facing a small box which sat on the floor next to the sink. It was hardly noticeable. He looked at Brooks and back to the box.

"This is it!" shouted Brooks. "Get that box off the plane!" Immediately, special bomb squad officers, dressed in protective clothing, carefully examined the box. They slowly placed it in a special container. Then they took it off the plane.

"Good boy, Bingo," Brooks said as he praised and patted the dog. From his pocket he took out Bingo's favorite toy. It was only a rolled-up towel, but he loved to play tug-o-war. The game was Bingo's reward after a "find."

In another part of the airport, the box was checked with care. A wrong move could make the bomb explode. Under some shredded newspapers, several pounds of plastic explosive were hidden. It was attached to a timer which was set to go off in fifteen minutes. The bomb was supposed to explode while the plane was in the air. The 242 passengers would have been killed.

"All in a day's work, Bingo," said Officer Brooks back in the patrol car. He scratched the dog behind his ears. The big shepherd closed his eyes. He napped all the way home.

Tom Iverson, and his narcotics detector dog, Dewey, work for the U.S. Customs Department.

12

2.

Law enforcement dogs in history

Since ancient times, dogs have been used to guard people and property. Dogs were first used on regular law enforcement patrols in the thirteenth century in France. They patrolled the dock areas in the port city of Saint-Malo.

Written records from fifteenth century England describe how bloodhounds were used to track down criminals. The city of Ghent, Belgium, started the first successful police working dog program in 1899. Soon, Germany, Switzerland, and other countries in Europe had similar law dog programs.

By 1920, the Germans had a special school which trained K-9's for law enforcement work. The dogs were taught obedience, tracking, searching, and controlled attack. Although New York City started a police dog program in 1907, it was not successful and ended in 1920. The program failed due to a shortage of good trainers, dogs, and funding.

After World War II, the city of London became a model for American K-9 programs. They were successfully using dogs on patrol to prevent crime. Baltimore, Maryland was the first city in America to start a K-9 program. It was in 1956. In its first year, two dogs were responsible for over five hundred arrests. Baltimore's program was so effective that other American cities followed with K-9 units of their own.

Today, hundreds of cities, both large and small, use dogs in law enforcement work. Some use one or two dogs. Others have over one hundred. K-9's also serve in the military police of the armed forces.

One of the most famous law dogs was a German shepherd named Dox. He worked for the Police Department in Rome, Italy. During his fifteen-year career, in the late forties and fifties, Dox caught hundreds of criminals. He also found more than one hundred lost children and saved dozens of people from drowning. He was shot seven times but lived to be nineteen years of age.

Today, dogs are trained to detect illegal contraband (forbidden foods and goods), narcotics, and explosives. They are called detector dogs. The United States Department of Agriculture uses detector dogs to locate fruits and meats being brought into the country. They sniff baggage at airports, border crossings, and post offices.

Since 1970, the United States Customs Service has used narcotics detector dogs to stop drug smuggling into the country. In 1983 alone, canine enforcement teams uncovered 3,245 cases of drug smuggling. The value of the drugs was over $261 million (U.S.). Narcotics detector dogs are also used by police departments throughout the country as well as the military police.

Since the early 1970's, explosives detector dogs have been used by police officials and law enforcement agencies to find hidden bombs. They have been used at airports throughout the U.S. by the Federal Aviation Agency (FAA) and the Law Enforcement Assistance Administration (LEAA). These dogs have saved many lives as well as hundreds of thousands of dollars of property.

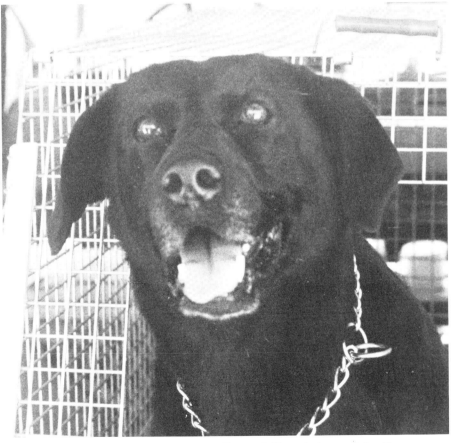

Dogs like Dewey help to stop the flow of illegal drugs into the United States.

3.

General requirements

Dogs used in law enforcement work must be intelligent, healthy, and strong. They are large, powerful dogs who are also agile and fast. Law dogs must be easily trained and respond to commands. They are under control at all times. They will stop an attack on command.

Law enforcement dogs are under control at all times.

Law dogs are loyal to their partners and protect them without question. They attack on their own only if their partners are attacked, if they are attacked, or if a suspect tries to escape. They are courageous, and ignore gunfire and other dangers. They are alert and willing to use their sense of smell. (All dogs have good scenting ability. Not all are willing to use it on command.)

Dogs are donated or bought by police departments and other agencies from people in the community, dog trainers, or kennels. Each department or agency differs from one another in age and size requirements for their dogs. Most are male dogs, usually about one to two years of age. (Males are used more often since they are larger and stronger than females.)

Several breeds of dogs have been used in law enforcement work over the years. However, the German shepherd is used more often than any other breed.

Detector dog requirements

Detector dogs must have a strong interest in retrieving. They have a natural desire to "fetch" an object and bring it back to their masters on command. They are intelligent and curious.

Detector dogs are easily trained and eager to please their handlers. They are even-tempered and energetic, but not too aggressive. Explosives detectors must be calm dogs and not get overly excited.

Dogs are often donated by or bought from individuals. However, the U.S. Customs Service gets most of their narcotics detector dogs from animal shelters around the country. The military police pick trained military patrol dogs who are above average in tracking, scouting, and searching. Police department detector dogs have all had basic police K-9 training.

Though most are male dogs, females can also be detector dogs, depending on the agency requirements. Age may differ from program to program. U.S. Customs dogs are one to two years of age. Other detector dogs may be as old as five years. Labrador retrievers, golden retrievers and German shepherds have all been successfully used as narcotics and explosives detector dogs.

German shepherds

Many believe the German shepherd is the best dog for work in law enforcement. The breed can be taught to attack with control. For years, these shepherd dogs of Germany were trained to herd and protect flocks of cattle and sheep. They learned to hold these animals with their mouths without hurting them.

The German shepherd has the size, strength, agility, and speed needed in police work. The shepherd has the courage and "heart" to go on, even if it's wounded or in pain. They are very loyal dogs, bred over the years to be a working partner to people.

German shepherds are intelligent and easily trained. They are powerful fighters. Shepherds have a bite equal to seven hundred pounds per square inch. They could easily break a person's arm. Yet the dog will only use enough force to hold the suspect until its partner can take over.

German shepherds are black, gray, brown, tan, and white. Many are a mixture of black with a lighter color. Males are twenty-four to twenty-six inches tall (60.96 - 66.04 cm) at the shoulders. They weigh between seventy-five and eighty-five pounds (34.02 - 38.56 kg). Females are twenty-two to twenty-four inches (55.88 - 60.96 cm) tall. They weigh between sixty and seventy pounds (27.22 - 31.75 kg).

German shepherds are the most popular dog for law enforcement.

Labradors and golden retrievers

Retrievers are dogs which were specially bred to bring back game during a hunt. The dogs would watch where the birds or animals fell. When the master gave the command, the dogs would bring the birds or animals back.

This natural retrieving drive is what makes these dogs good narcotics or explosives detectors.

Labrador retrievers are black, yellow, or chocolate colored. The yellow labs range from fox-red to a cream color. They have short, straight, thick coats. Male Labradors are 22½ to 24½ inches tall (57.15 - 62.23 cm) at the shoulder. Females are 21½ to 23½ inches (54.61 - 59.69 cm) tall. Labradors weigh between fifty-five and seventy-five pounds (24.95 - 34.02 kg).

Golden retrievers are a yellow-gold color which comes in many shades. Some are creamy white. Others are deep-red. They have fringes of hair (called feathering) on the back of their front legs. Feathering is also on the neck, under the tail, and on the back of the thighs.

Male golden retrievers are twenty-three to twenty-four inches (58.42 - 60.96 cm) tall at the shoulder. They weigh sixty-five to seventy-five pounds (29.48 - 34.02 kg). Females are 21½ to 22½ inches tall (54.61 - 57.15 cm) and weigh sixty to seventy pounds (27.22 - 31.75 kg).

4.
Why use dogs?

Many people believe dogs help prevent crime. They may cause more fear to people than guns. A large, snarling animal, ready to attack, discourages lawbreakers. Dogs can take the place of a police officer on patrol and they are less expensive. They aid and protect their partners. They do not kill. An attacking dog can be stopped by a command. But a bullet from a gun cannot be ordered back.

Dogs can be taught to attack on command.

The dog's sharp senses let them search buildings and other areas faster and more completely than their human partners. They can track criminals by scent. Their speed and agility lets them go places where their partners can't go.

Types of programs

The goals of all K-9 law enforcement training programs are the same. Dogs are trained to assist their human partners in enforcing the law, catching criminals, and preventing crime. However, each local police department or law enforcement agency may be different

A law enforcement dog learns to attack.

in the type and length of training for dogs and handlers. They also may differ in how and where they get their dogs.

Many police departments work with their own local governments to start a K-9 program. Dogs are often donated to the program by individuals. Sometimes money is raised to buy dogs by service clubs and businesses. Some police departments get their dogs from local trainers or kennels who breed dogs just for work in law enforcement.

After visiting successful K-9 programs, other police departments in large cities have set up their own training programs. Many get their dogs from Germany where they are specially bred for police work. The dogs are already fully-trained and obey commands in German. The handlers are then trained to work with the dog, usually for about three to four weeks. Training may continue once a week for up to a year.

Basic training for new law dogs takes about fourteen weeks for most programs. Some police K-9 officers attend private dog training schools with their animals. The Central Florida Criminal Justice Regional Training Center, in Orlando, is a basic police dog school run by the state of Florida. Advanced training for narcotics and explosives detector dogs at Orlando may take another four weeks.

Military police patrol and detector dogs are trained by the Air Force at Lackland Air Force Base in Texas for all the armed services. U.S. Customs Service narcotics detector dogs are trained for fourteen weeks at the Canine Enforcement Training Center at Front Royal, Virginia.

Handlers

Dog handlers in police departments are experienced officers. They enjoy caring for and working with dogs. The dogs live at home with their partners. Off-duty, the dog is just a gentle, family pet.

Handlers spend much of their free time caring for the dog. It becomes a member of the family. A bond grows between the officer and K-9. The dogs become very loyal and protective of their partners. The officers become very attached to the dogs.

U.S. Customs Canine Enforcement officers are selected from employees of the U.S. Customs Service. Each officer is assigned two dog partners at the training center. About sixty percent of the dogs complete the training. Those who are dropped from the program are usually adopted by people in the community.

If both dogs pass the training, the officer picks one of them to be a working partner. The other dog is then reassigned to another handler. Then the dog team is assigned to a duty station. The dog lives in a local kennel. Each handler picks up the K-9 in the morning and drives to work. The dog rides in a wire cage in the back of a station wagon. Then it works with the

The dogs usually ride in wire cages in the back of a vehicle.

handler during the day. After a run at the end of work, the dog is returned to its kennel for the night.

Military police dog handlers are all volunteers. They must take and pass a patrol dog handler training course. Detector dog handlers are volunteers who are qualified patrol dog handlers with a least one year of experience.

The handlers are all volunteers.

Selecting dogs

Dogs donated to police and military police programs are tested to see if they qualify as law dogs. Testing may differ from program to program. First a dog must be aggressive (ready to attack) toward a stranger who teases it. Very shy or overly aggressive dogs are not selected.

Next a dog must not be gun-shy. A person fires blanks from a gun into the air to test the dog's reaction. Over-excited, nervous, or frightened dogs are not selected.

The U.S. Customs Service select their narcotics detector dogs by giving them a series of retrieving tests. The dog must have a desire to fetch and play with a toy. A white towel is the toy used in U.S. Customs training. The handler throws the towel. If the dog is not interested in getting it, bringing it back to the handler, or playing tug-o-war, the dog will not pass. The handler may throw the towel inside or under a car. If the dog goes to retrieve it, the dog passes the test. Dogs should be even-tempered, full of energy, and friendly. Growling, over-aggressive dogs are not selected. Only about one dog in forty-five pass the Customs tests.

Basic training

The Central Florida Training Center in Orlando offers a basic police dog program for dogs and handlers.

Other training schools have similar programs.

At Central Florida, the dog and handler work five days a week for eight hours each day. Handlers learn about dog behavior and the parts of the canine body. Veterinarians talk about how to care for the dog. The handler grooms and feeds the dog. Each day the dog and handler take a ten-mile walk together. Handlers are taught training methods and how to break up dogfights. They learn how to lift their K-9's and how to use their equipment and keep it in good condition.

Rewards and corrections

The dogs are trained by repeating commands and the use of praise or corrections. When the dog is correct, it gets either spoken praise ("good boy or girl") or physical praise (a pat or rub). If a dog is not correct, it doesn't get praised. The handler may say "no" or jerk on the dog's leash. The handler must always be patient with the dog and never lose control.

Obedience training

Obedience commands are taught to the dog by the handler while it is on the leash. These sessions are fifteen minutes long with five minute breaks between sessions. The handler and dog learn both spoken and

The basic command is "heel."

hand commands. The basic command is "heel." The
dog is trained to walk, stand, or sit at its handler's left
side. The hand command for "heel" is slapping the left
leg with an open left hand. In the heel-sit, the dog sits
beside the handler's left leg. The hand command for
"sit" is the right arm raised with palm up.

Other obedience commands taught are "stay,"
"down," and "come." The command "take cover"
is taught for protection. The command "crawl" is given
when the dog is in the "down" position. The handler
always praises the dog after each exercise is done
correctly.

The next part of obedience training is learning and practicing commands at a distance. The dog responds to all spoken and hand commands while on a twenty-five foot leash. Then handlers practice the exercise while the dog is off the leash. The distance is slowly increased until the handler is sure of complete control over the dog. Finally, the obedience exercises are done in areas where there are other people and many distractions for the dog.

Agility

During the fourth and fifth weeks of training, the K-9's begin agility work. The dogs begin jumping over

Dogs learn to jump a variety of obstacles.

hurdles. The height of the hurdles is slowly increased. The dog learns to jump through a ring of fire and over an eight-foot wall. They climb up ladders, crawl through pipes, and jump out car doors. The dogs usually enjoy the agility course and look forward to the activity. It exposes the dog to different situations they may have to face while on the job.

Attack training

By the eighth week, controlled attack training begins. The police K-9 must watch, chase, attack, and hold on to someone on command from the handler. One of the trainers wears a padded sleeve and carries a small stick

When given the command, "hold him," the dog hangs on.

or burlap bag. This person is the "agitator." The agitator's job is to annoy the dog and wave the stick or bag at it.

Dogs and handlers line up facing the agitator. The dogs are on the leash. The agitator begins teasing one of the dogs. Its handler says "watch him." The dog should get very excited, watching every move of the agitator. Then the handler says "get him." This is the signal to attack. The agitator lets the dog bite the sack or padded sleeve. Once the dog bites, the handler quickly says "hold him." The dog should hold on firmly and not let go.

With the command "out, heel," the dog lets go and returns to the heel position. This is practiced again and again in a line or circle formation. Soon, with corrections, the dog will understand what is expected of it. The agitator slowly moves farther away. The dog begins to follow the commands, "watch him," "get him," "hold him," and "out, heel," while off the leash.

Gunfire — protecting the handler

The dog must learn to follow commands while under fire. The agitator stands thirty yards away from the dog and handler. As the dog team walks closer, the agitator starts running and fires a gunshot. The handler says "get him." The agitator fires more shots. The dog should chase and attack the agitator, ignoring the gunshots. Then the handler says "out, heel," and the dog should stop the attack and return.

The handler tells the dog to "stay" and moves alone toward the agitator. The handler starts to search the agitator. Suddenly, the agitator hits the handler, who falls down. Seeing this, the dog should attack on its own to protect the handler. At first, the handler may have to use the command "get him." After practicing, the dog will learn to attack on its own. Once the dog attacks, the handler says "out, heel" and it returns to the handler's side.

Again, the handler commands "stay" and goes to search the agitator. Then the handler walks five feet behind the agitator and says "come, heel." The dog should be able to walk by the agitator into the heel position without attacking.

In other exercises, the agitator stands twenty yards from the dog team. The dog is commanded to "stay." Then the agitator runs ten yards and stops. The dog should keep still and not move. Next, the agitator starts to run but he doesn't stop. The dog is given the attack command and chases the agitator. Then the dog is called back from the attack. The handler says "come," or "out, heel."

Special attack situations, such as more than one agitator, are practiced many times until they become automatic for the dog and officer. The dog learns to ignore clubs, knives, and other weapons. The dog will try to go for the agitator's arm but will attack other parts of the body if necessary. Dogs who won't bite, or are too friendly, are dropped from the program. (If they are otherwise good dogs, especially in searching and tracking, they may be used as narcotics or explosives detectors, depending on the program.)

While attack, agility, and obedience practice continues, retrieving work begins. The K-9 and handler work on the dog retrieving articles with a human scent on them. The dog is taught to bring back articles such as handguns, wallets, keys, and matchbooks in any given area. The command "find it" is used by the handler.

Building search

By the tenth week of training, work begins on building searches. An agitator teases the dog and runs into a building. The dog and handler chase the agitator, on a leash, up to the door of the building. The officer shouts, "This is a canine unit from ___ Department. If you do not come out, I'll release my dog." At the command "search" or "find him" the K-9 is let off the leash and enters the building to find the agitator.

When the dog finds the person, the handler commands "get him." After the dog grabs the padded sleeve and holds the agitator, "out, heel" is commanded. The dog returns to the handler's side. The handler then commands, ''watch him'' or ''stay'' and goes to search the agitator.

The agitator hits the handler. The K-9 should attack and hold the agitator on its own to protect its partner. The handler then commands ''out, heel.'' The exercise ends when the dog team walks with the agitator out of the building. By watching the dog carefully during the

This German shepherd is being trained to search a building.

search, the handler will learn how the dog alerts. Its hair may rise up on its back. It may growl. All dogs are different.

In the advanced building search, one or two agitators will already be hidden somewhere in the building. Neither the dog nor the handler know where. The handler shouts the warning and then releases the dog. The handler stands just inside the door to give the dog time to find the agitators. If the dog has trouble, the handler will command it to "search" certain areas.

After a time, night problems are given. Handlers learn how the dog's nose works. They learn how air currents affect the search. Then field searches are practiced with cross trails and two agitators. Search problems are slowly made more difficult for the dog.

This dog is looking for a scent trail.

Tracking

The dog "searches" by following the air scents of people. When the tracking harness and leash are put on, the dog is taught to follow ground scents. It learns to connect the harness with tracking.

New commands are given to the dog. The Central Florida program uses "suche suche" (pronounced sook) when a dog is trying to find the track. This means "track" in German. Other programs may use the command "track," "find," or "seek." "Suche suche" may also be used when the dog is confused or is trying to get back on the track after losing it.

"Suche on" is given when the dog finds the track. It's also used to encourage the dog. If the dog starts to

The dog has found a person hiding in a tree.

leave the track and is distracted, the handler says "no—leave it" and then "suche suche" or "suche on." "Easy" is said to slow up the dog's speed while tracking.

First the handler puts the tracking harness on the K-9. Then the leash is handed to an instructor. The handler walks in a straight line about fifty yards downwind of the dog. The dog is put in a "down" position. The instructor commands "suche suche." The dog should pick up the scent trail and move toward the handler. When the K-9's nose is on the track, the instructor says "suche on." Sometimes fish or spoiled food is dragged along the track. This helps the weaker dogs keep their nose to the ground.

When the dog gets to the handler the harness is taken off and the dog is praised. These exercises are repeated with the handler walking longer distances away. After a time, the dog should be able to find the handler on a three hundred yard, twenty-minute-old track. Next the handler and dog learn to follow the track of a stranger. The length and age of the track is slowly increased and turns are added.

In advanced tracking, the dog team follows an unknown, one-mile long soft track (in a wooded area) which is one hour old. It has two turns and a cross track mixed in to make it harder. These advanced exercises also take place on hard concrete surfaces (called a hard track) in populated areas. Some night problems are also given.

Advanced training — narcotics

The U.S. Customs Canine Enforcement Program trains narcotics detector dogs which have a very strong desire to play fetch. The dog searches for drugs because it enjoys it. These dogs do not receive obedience or attack training like police or military police detector dogs.

According to Chuck Truax, Program Manager for the Customs Canine Program in Los Angeles, a special retrieve article, such as a rolled-up towel, is scented

An article, such as a towel, is used to familiarize the dog with a narcotics smell.

with a narcotics smell. The game of fetch is played with the dog. Soon the dog learns to connect the smell of the drug with its toy.

Next, the dog's toy is hidden. The handler tells the dog to "fetch" or "find" the toy. The dog searches for it by using its scenting powers. The Customs dogs are trained to bite or scratch at anything that comes between it and the narcotics. In the dog's mind, it's searching for the toy. The biting and scratching alerts the handler. The handler takes the toy, which is kept

After finding narcotics, the dog is given his "toy" as a reward.

hidden in a coat or pocket, and puts it near the narcotic so the dog can get it. This is its reward. The dogs practice finding narcotics in cars, aircraft, ships, baggage, boxes, packages, and in mail.

At the Central Florida Training Center, narcotics detector dogs have already passed basic police K-9 training. The dog is introduced to the smell of narcotics by scenting a canvas packet with drugs. This is used as the dog's play toy. The dog plays fetch games with the toy. Then a scent discrimination box is used. This is a box made of wood and about five feet long. It has separate sections. The narcotic is put into one of these sections. The handler says "seek." The dog goes past the box sniffing all the sections. When the dog sniffs the section with the drugs, the handler encourages it to get very excited and praises it. The dog's toy is given as a reward. After repeated practice, the dog under-stands how it is suppose to act. It looks forward to the praise and the toy reward.

Next, the narcotic is placed in different hiding places such as lockers, cars, airplanes, or boats. It's hidden in boxes, suitcases, canvas bags, plastic bags, or film containers. The handler makes each practice harder. To keep up the dog's interest, the areas to be searched are changed.

Then masking agents are introduced. This is anything that can be used to try and hide the smell of the drug. Perfume, oregano, pepper, and detergent are masking agents. The fully-trained K-9 is expected to find a narcotic, "even if it's hidden under a towel soaked with perfume," says Robert Cook, Canine Instructor at the Florida Training Center.

Records are kept on the dog's finds and misses. If the dog begins to miss a certain percentage, it goes through retraining. It should be correct more than ninety percent of the time. Military police narcotics detector dogs are trained in a similar way. Usually a rubber ball or a small canvas bag is used as the dog's toy reward.

Advanced training — explosives

Explosives detector dogs are trained in almost the same way as narcotics detector dogs. There is one main difference. The explosives detector is trained to always sit quietly when it alerts. It must not touch the explosives it discovers. Sometimes, explosives dogs are trained to bark, depending on the program. When the dog alerts correctly, it is rewarded with praise and its favorite fetch toy, a rubber ball or towel.

These K-9's are trained to detect explosives such as black powder, TNT, Flex-X, C-4 plastic, and a Gel explosive. Since they work around dangerous material, the dogs must have calm and even temperaments.

At the beginning of training, the toy of the explosives detector dog is **not** scented with explosives. They are

The dog is always praised when it alerts correctly.

introduced to the smell with the use of a scent discrimination box. Once the dog sniffs and shows interest in
the section which holds the explosive, the handler puts
the dog into a sit position. Then the handler praises it
and gives the dog its toy as a reward. After repeated
practices, the dog will automatically sit when it detects
the odor of explosives and wait for its reward.

5.

Training never stops

U.S. Customs dogs can work from eight to ten years if they stay in good health and are effective in detecting narcotics. When they retire, the dogs may become a pet of the handler or be placed in a good home.

Police K-9's average about six years of work. They are under more stressful and dangerous situations each day. These dogs are almost always kept by their human partners as family pets once they retire.

Dogs are often tested once a year to be sure their skill levels are at a high level. A dog which begins to work poorly on the job or test low may have to be retrained.

Continous training (at least once a week for a few

Law enforcement dogs need to train a few hours every week.

hours) is important to keep the skills of the law dog at a high level. Detector dogs practice with different narcotics and explosives problems set up by their handler. Police K-9's may practice tracking or searching. Some K-9 teams practice to take part in the police dog trials held each year.

The National Police Dog Trials are sponsored by the U.S. Police Canine Association. The trials decide which is the best police dog in the country. First the dogs are judged on obedience and agility. In the search category, the K-9 has a few minutes to find hidden articles in high grass and return them to its handler. Next, the dog must find a person hidden in one of six large boxes within a few minutes time. The dogs are also judged in attack and capture situations, gun attacks, and how it protects its handler.

Benefits and costs

Police K-9 teams patrol on foot and in cars. They track down suspects, capture criminals, and search buildings and other areas. They've been used for crowd and riot control. More and more cities each year are using dogs to assist their police officers. In many high crime areas, purse-snatchings, attacks, and holdups have lowered when dog teams are used in the area.

Narcotics detector dogs can check a car or truck for drugs in five or six minutes. A Customs inspector needs at least twenty minutes to do the same thing. A dog team can check over four hundred to five hundred packages in thirty minutes. The accuracy rate of the explosives detector dogs is better then ninety-five percent. When time is so important, these dogs can detect explosives in a fraction of the time it would take their human partners.

The cost of a trained police K-9 can be as much as five or six thousand dollars (U.S.). This depends on whether the dog is purchased, already trained, or donated. The savings to a community in terms of man-hours and crime prevention is hard to figure. The price of a trained law dog is small compared to lowering the crime rate, catching lawbreakers, or saving the life of an officer or citizen.

Dogs have been successful in all areas of law enforcement. Their scenting powers, strength, speed, and intelligence have helped to discourage crime wherever and whenever they are used.

Glossary

AGITATOR — *A person who stirs things up; excites or moves quickly.*

CUSTODY — *To arrest; to keep under guard by the police.*

EXPLOSIVES — *A material or substance that can explode or blowup.*

HARD TRACK — *A ground scent trail on concrete or other hard surface areas.*

K-9 — *A term for dog (canine); refers to dogs active in police or military service.*

MASKING AGENT — *Anything that can be used to try and hide the smell of narcotics and explosives.*

NARCOTICS — *Drugs; narcotics detector dogs find illegal drugs such as marijuana, cocaine, or heroin.*

OREGANO — *Leaves of plants of the mint family used in seasoning food; sometimes used as a masking agent.*

SCENT DISCRIMINATION BOX — *A five-foot-long, wooden box divided into separate sections or compartments; a narcotic or explosive is placed in one section for dogs to practice detection.*

SEARCH — *Command used in buildings and field areas; the dog follows the air scents to find people.*

SECURITY — *Safety, free from danger, protection.*

SOFT TRACK — *A ground scent trail in a wooded or other soft surface area.*

SUCHE ON — *A command in tracking; used when the dog finds the track; also used to encourage the dog (pronounced sook).*

SUCHE SUCHE — *Means "track" in German; command in tracking which is used when the dog is trying to find the track (pronounced sook).*

SUSPECT — *A person who is believed to be guilty of a crime.*

TEMPERAMENT — *The emotional characteristics that are special to each dog; its personality or frame of mind.*

TRACKING — *The dog follows the ground scents to find people.*

VETERINARIAN — *A doctor who treats animals.*

*READ ABOUT THE MANY KINDS
OF DOGS THAT WORK FOR A LIVING:*

**HEARING-EAR
DOGS**

**GUIDE
DOGS**

**WATCH/GUARD
DOGS**

**LAW
ENFORCEMENT
DOGS**

**SEARCH
& RESCUE
DOGS**

**STUNT
DOGS**

**SLED
DOGS**

**MILITARY
DOGS**

CRESTWOOD HOUSE